Maps

LEVEL 11

DECODABLES

BY jump!

Teaching Tips

Lime Level 11

This book focuses on developing reading independence, fluency, and comprehension.

Before Reading

- Ask readers what they think the book will be about based on the title. Have them support their answer.

Read the Book

- Encourage readers to read silently on their own.
- As readers encounter unfamiliar words, ask them to look for context clues to see if they can figure out what the words mean. Encourage them to locate boldfaced words in the glossary and ask questions to clarify the meaning of new vocabulary.
- Allow readers time to absorb the text and think about each chapter.
- Ask readers to write down any questions they have about the book's content.

After Reading

- Ask readers to summarize the book.
- Encourage them to point out anything they did not understand and ask questions.
- Ask readers to review the questions on page 23. Have them go back through the book to find answers. Have them write their answers on a separate sheet of paper.

5357 Penn Avenue South
Minneapolis, MN 55419
www.jumplibrary.com

Decodables by Jump! are published by Jump! Library.

Library of Congress Cataloging-in-Publication Data is available at www.loc.gov or upon request from the publisher.

ISBN: 979-8-88524-820-4 (hardcover)
ISBN: 979-8-88524-821-1 (paperback)
ISBN: 979-8-88524-822-8 (ebook)

Photo Credits

Images are courtesy of Shutterstock.com. With thanks to Getty Images, Thinkstock Photo and iStockphoto. Cover – Krakenimages.com. p4–5 – Prostock-studio, Aris-Tect Group. p6–7 – WDG Photo, Rainer Lesniewski. p8–9 – george studio, Daniel Chetroni. p10–11 – Dmitry Kalinovsky, Teo Angelovski. p12–13 – Carlos Amarillo, Rawpixel.com. p14–15 –Rainer Lesniewski, Vitalii Matokha. p16–17 – Marzolino, Calvivs. p18–19 – Haider Y. Abdulla, AndreyPopov. p20–21 – frees, Porcupen.

Table of Contents

What Are Maps?

Maps are often drawings that show parts of the world and how they are connected. Maps can show a big area, such as the entire world, or a small area, such as a town or city. Some maps only show natural features of the landscape, such as mountains and rivers. Other maps show where buildings and roads are.

Maps are a way of showing information. Some maps, such as road maps, show information that helps people find their way from one place to another, but not all maps are made for traveling. Maps are also used to show information about **landmarks**, animals, or people. A person who makes maps is called a cartographer.

World map

Mapping Local Areas

It is important to map towns and cities so that the people who live there or tourists who come to visit know how to get around. Maps are great for giving directions and can help you find important landmarks and places to go. Maps of local areas are also used to plan new buildings.

The Eiffel Tower is an important landmark.

New York City is one of the largest cities in the world. Because it is so big, it is split into smaller areas called boroughs. The boroughs are called Manhattan, Brooklyn, Queens, Staten Island, and the Bronx. Each borough has its own map with more detail.

Map of New York City

What Does a Town Map Look Like?

Maps are drawn from a bird's-eye view. This means they are drawn as if looking down at an area from above like a bird would. Bird's-eye views of towns and cities help us see how close we are to other places. Maps of towns and cities use **symbols** to show where things are.

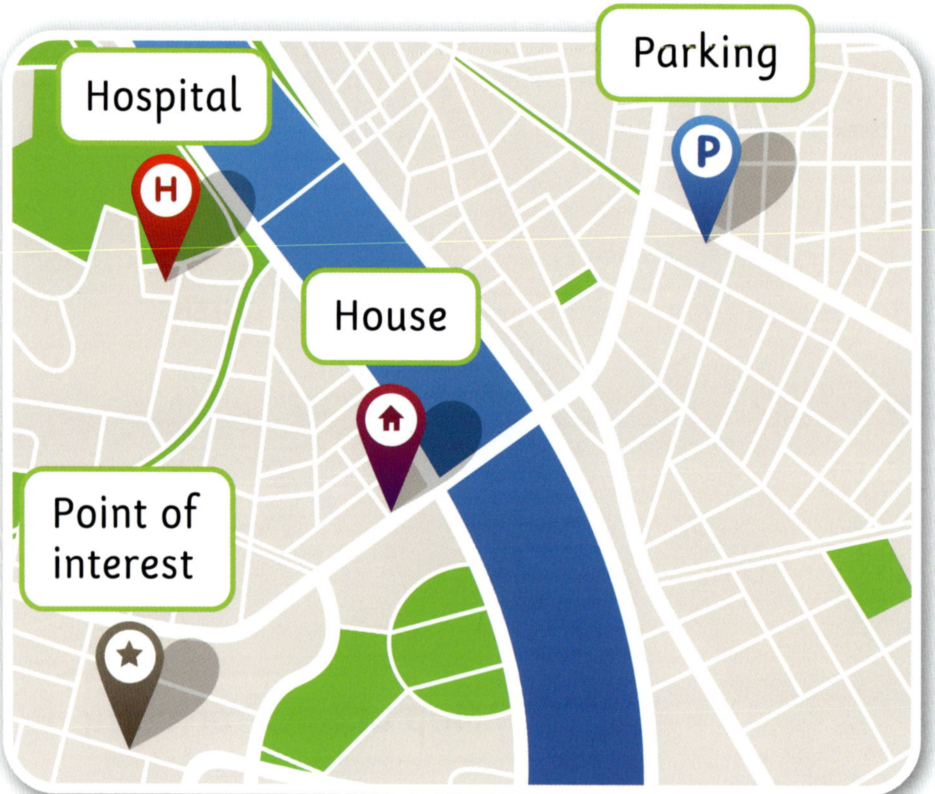

As well as symbols, maps of towns and cities also use color codes. **Color coding** is especially useful for road maps, as it can help drivers tell the difference between types of roads. The road map of London below is color coded so drivers can plan their routes in and out of the city.

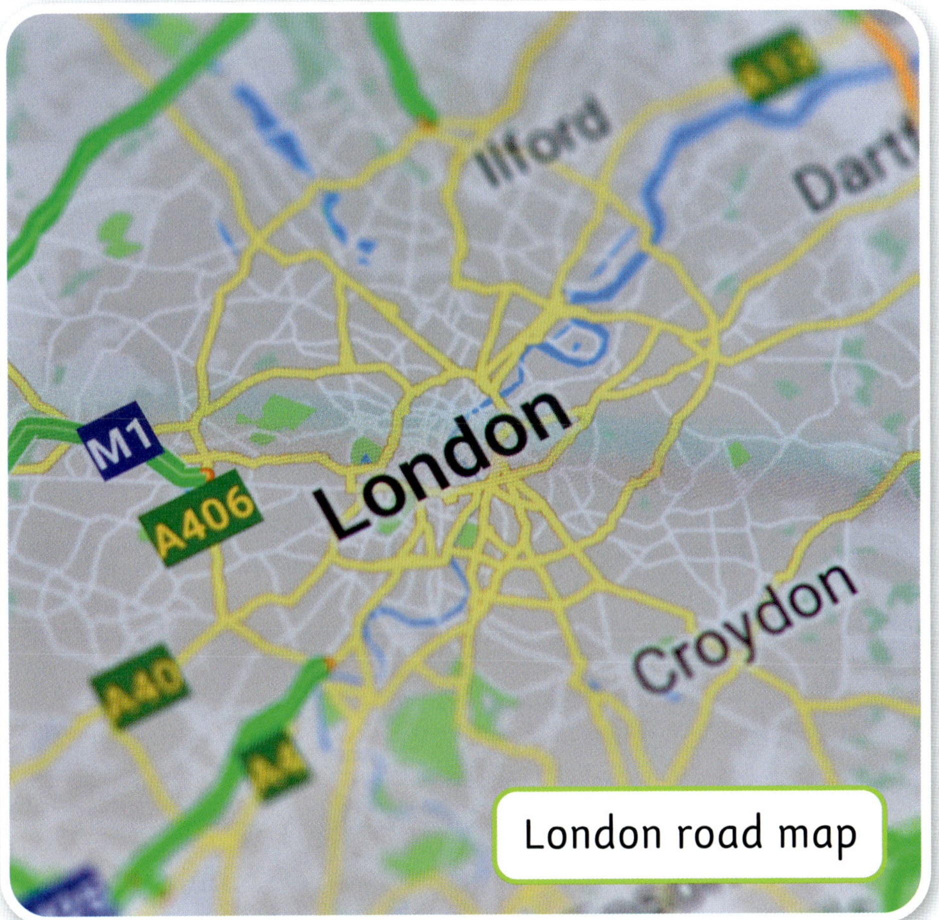

London road map

How City Maps Are Made

Mapmaking is called cartography. Cartography has a very long history. Some of the earliest maps of towns and cities were made by climbing to the top of a tall mountain or building and sketching the area. This is called surveying. Surveying is done by surveyors, and they have to be very careful to get it exactly right.

Surveyor

Airplanes and helicopters allow us to take photos of landscapes from very high up. This gives us a much better view of where everything is. We also use satellite technology to create maps. Satellites are human-made objects that orbit Earth and take images and collect information. Maps today are more **accurate** than ever before.

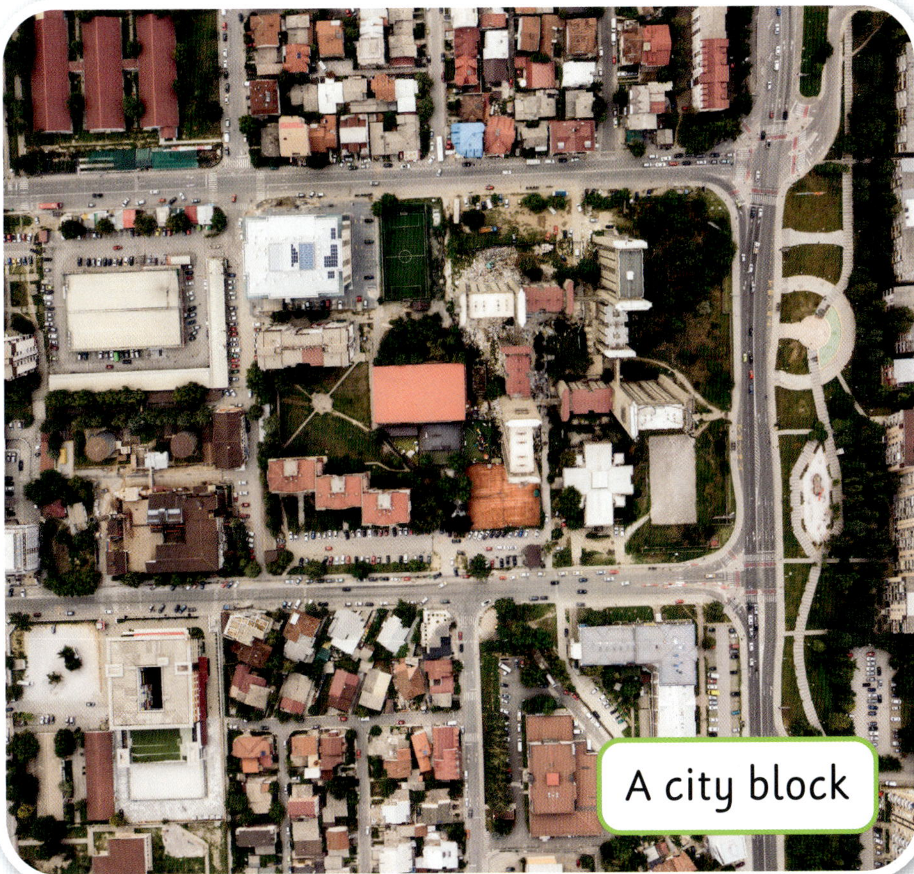

A city block

Using a Compass

Maps also have a drawing of a **compass**, called a **compass rose**, printed on them. This tells you which way is north, south, east, and west on the map. If you are going south, it can help to turn the map upside down so that it matches the direction you are facing.

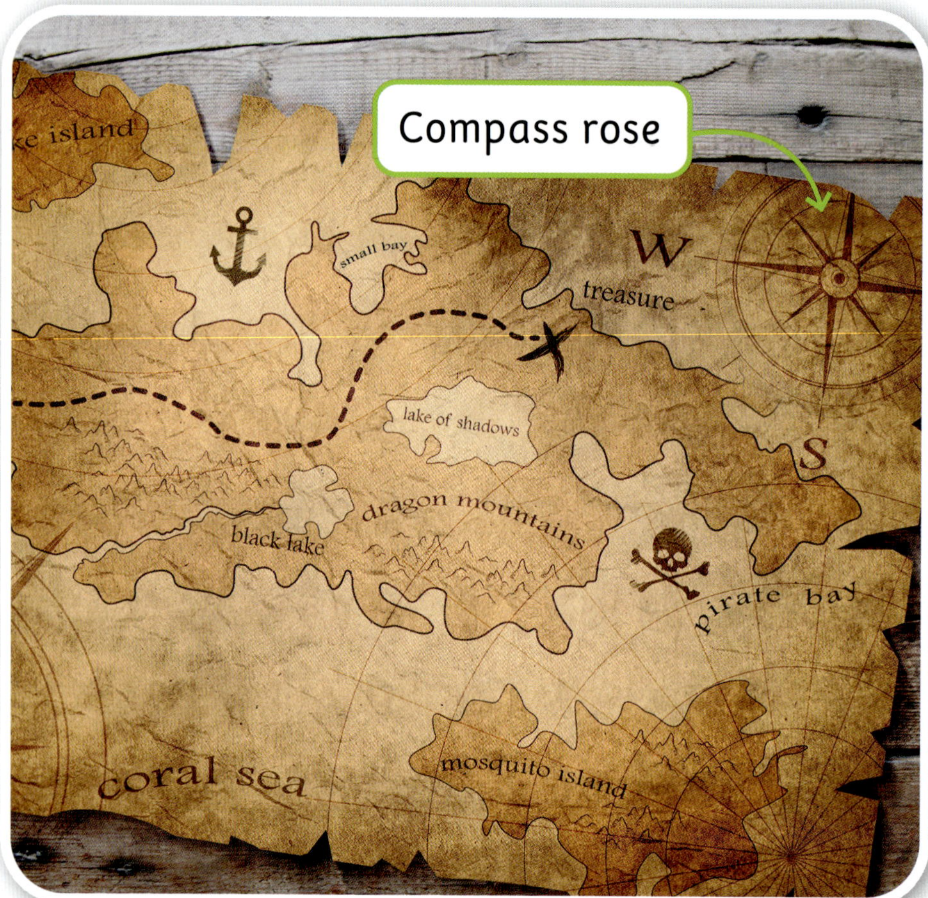

It can be hard to know which direction you are facing without a real compass. To use a compass, you should hold it still and flat in the palm of your hand. Wherever the needle points is north, even if it doesn't line up with the "N" on the compass dial.

Landscapes

Topographic maps show the terrain of an area, which means the different parts of its landscape, such as forests or grass plains. They also show the height differences between areas. The height of an area, known as its elevation, is measured from sea level. The slopes around an area of elevation are shown using lines.

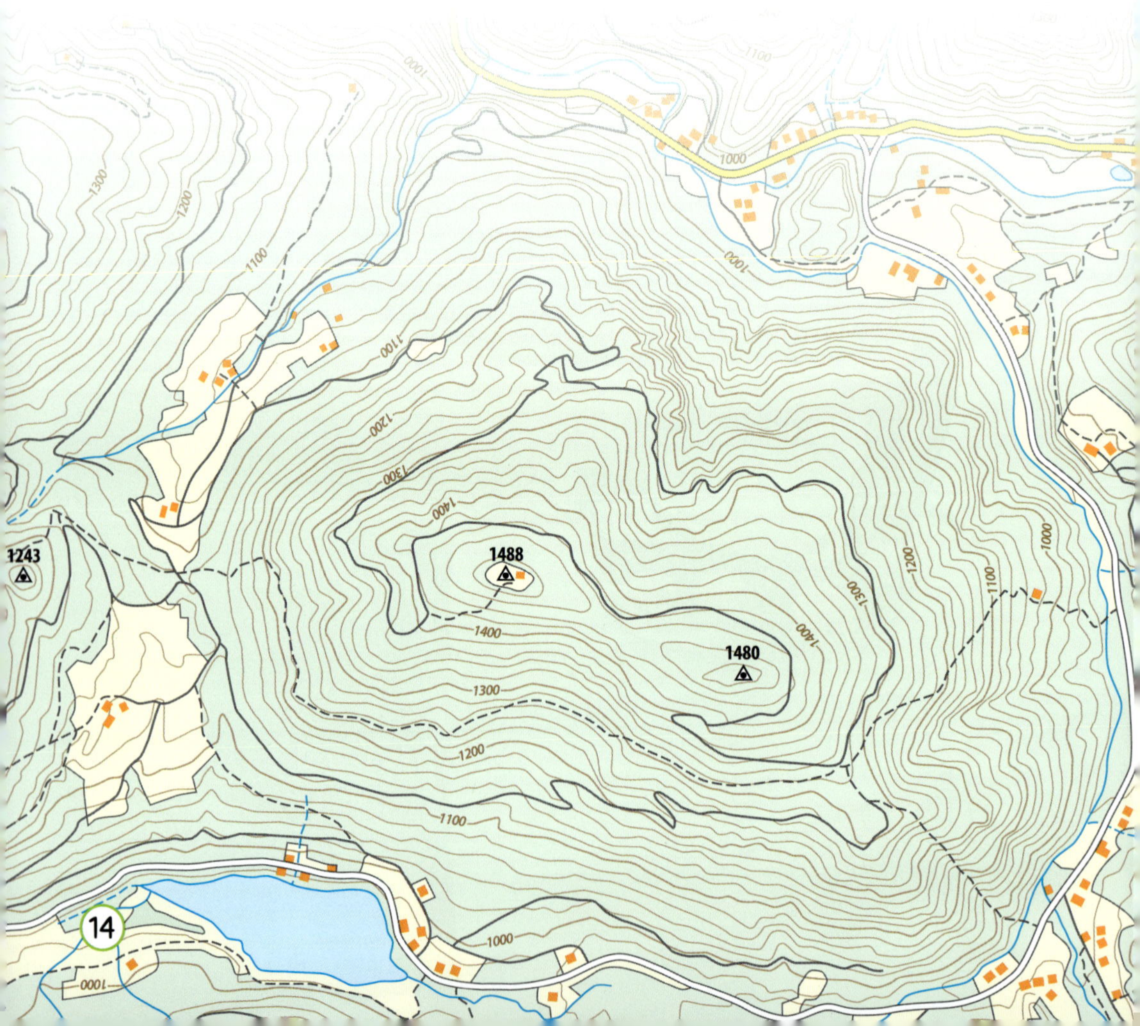

A topographic map can help travelers plan a trip by telling them where all the hills or rivers are. A topographic map will also show travelers when the way ahead is impossible to get through. For example, a mountain range could block your route. By checking a topographic map, travelers can wear and pack the right gear they will need for their trip.

Early Maps

Old maps tell us how much the people who made them knew about the world they lived in. For example, North and South America don't appear on ancient Roman maps, so we know they hadn't discovered either of these places.

Until 600 years ago, maps were hand-drawn, so they were rare. This meant many people had never seen one.

How we make and read maps has changed over time. Before 1569, maps of Earth were usually shown on round globes. A mapmaker named Gerardus Mercator made the first flat map of the world, which helped sailors plan their journeys.

We still use globes to this day.

Size and Scale

Scale is how the real size of something matches up with the size it is shown on a map. For example, one inch on a map can be used to show one mile in real life. The area that is being drawn needs to be shrunk to fit on the map.

Using a scale to draw anything that is real and measurable makes the drawing more accurate. Architects are people who plan buildings. They use scale drawings to show exactly how their planned building will look. A large-scale map shows a lot of detail. A small-scale map has a smaller amount of detail and shows a wider area.

Grids

Some places, such as hills or fields that do not have addresses, can be hard to find even with a map. This is why maps have **grids**. Each point on a map has grid numbers to help people count how horizontal (side to side) and how vertical (up and down) something is on a map.

People can find exactly where something on a map is by using the grid. A grid over a world map is like a grid over a town map but can be used to find any place on Earth. If you tell someone the numbers of the nearest horizontal and vertical lines to where you are, known as your coordinates, they can easily find you.

Index

How to Use an Index

An index helps us find information in a book. Each word has a set of page numbers. These page numbers are where you can find information about that word.

Page numbers

Example: balloons 5, 8–10, 19

Important word

This means page 8, page 10,
and all the pages in between.
Here, it means pages 8, 9, and 10.

Questions

1. What type of view are maps drawn from?
    a. Bird's-eye view
    b. Cat's-eye view
    c. Worm's-eye view

2. Which direction does a compass needle point to?
    a. West
    b. East
    c. North
    d. South

3. What is mapmaking also called?

4. Can you use the Table of Contents to find out how maps are made?

5. Can you use the Index to find information about New York City in this book?

6. Using the Glossary, can you define what symbols are?

Glossary

accurate:
Correct in details.

color coding:
Using colors to represent things or places.

compass:
An instrument with a magnetic pointer that always points north and is used for finding directions.

compass rose:
A circle showing directions printed on a map.

grids:
A network of evenly spaced horizontal and vertical lines that forms a regular pattern of squares.

landmarks:
Objects in a landscape that stand out.

scale:
The ratio between the measurements on a map and the actual, real-life measurements.

symbols:
Designs or objects that stand for something else.